Unveiled Anthems: A Symphony of Women's Voices

Unveiled Anthems: A Symphony of Women's Voices

Authors:
Monette Rockliff, Jasmine Woodsen, Jessamyn Stewart, Kelsey Klip,
L. Vallada, Stevie Mud, Afrah Collier, Grace Fay, Brooklyn Trapp, Afton Doe,
Sabryn Jones, Gillian Peacock, Alexis Virus, Rebecca Ryan, Teresa Dorey,
Kayla Hastings, J.Hildebrandt, Isabelle Desrochers-Stein, Lena Parnell,
CEDARS, Tanjeryne, Zoii Topia, Charlene Smith, Carla Rae Taylor, Jaide
Chyzyk, Nadine EL-Hajj, Sophia Ocean, Kavita Sundar, Amani Assaf

Edited by
Austin Mardon
Catherine Mardon
Josh Harnack

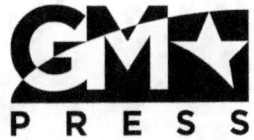

Copyright © 2023 by Austin Mardon

All rights reserved. This book or any portion thereof may not be reproduced or used in any manner whatsoever without the express written permission of the publisher except for the use of brief quotations in a book review or scholarly journal.

First Printing: 2023

Typeset, Cover Design and Illustrations by
Monette Rockliff & Josh Harnack

ISBN: 978-1-77889-047-5
eBook ISBN: 978-1-77889-048-2

Golden Meteorite Press
103 11919 82 St NW
Edmonton, AB T5B 2W3
www.goldenmeteoritepress.com

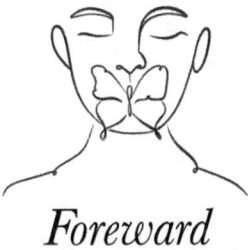

Foreward

The following is a collection of poetry from numerous women all over North America. These are our unfiltered, unedited, and vulnerable expressions. May one of these expressions land in your heart and may you feel inspired to have the courage to be heard and seen in whatever it is your soul needs.

A very special thank you to each and every woman who contributed to this book.

This book contains content that might be triggering to some readers, including, but not limited to references of rape, abortion, self-harm and abuse.

Please read with caution

Unveiled Anthems:

One size does NOT fit all

I live in a world that wants to keep me small

You feel too much!
You express too much!
You talk too much!
You ask for too much!

Be quiet, sit still
Do as your told, cross your legs
And don't you dare take up so much space

So then let me ask you something
Where do I fit in?
Where do I go?
So that I'm not squeezing my feet into shoes
That are two sizes too small?

Where can I be the way "God" intended me to be?
Where can I kick and scream
And say whatever the fuck I mean?

Am I too much for society?
Or is society made only as
A one size fits all
To keep us all so very small?

Each fingertip is completely unique
So why can't I honour what is uniquely me?

Is it me that doesn't fit into society,
Or is society just too small for me

Monette Rockliff

The question's only rhetoric

If my words float through time
Without reason or rhyme
If they fail to move and delight

Do I have permission to write?

If I sing out of tune
Melodically misguided
The critics divided

Will my voice be rightfully silenced?

If the sway of my hips
And mistimed dips
Seem rhythmless in their bliss

May I dance in spite of this?

Gillian Peacock

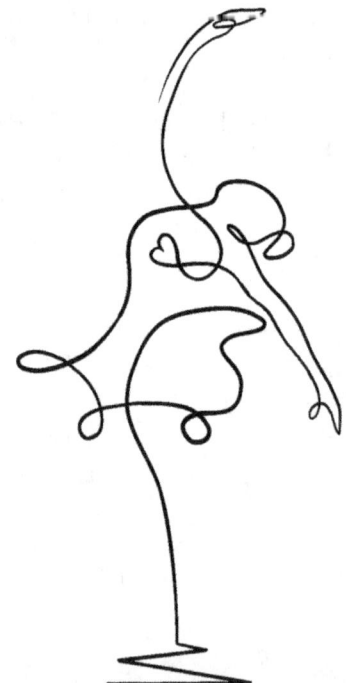

Sexy

Sexy
This word would not be said to me before my late 20's.
A word I let hold so much power over me.
As if I were the marionette and those were my strings
Cute, Adorable, Sweet
The same words used to describe a baby used to embrace me
The power of these words taring at my sanity
Comparing myself to those who stood around me
I am not enough
I am not the goddess divine, wrapping her spindle-like fingers weaving webs within your mind
Sexy
A word used to anchor me in the depths of self apathy
A word that I let tell me whom I could be
You see the idea of being desired, worshipped, idolized even lit a small part of my being that craved that validation
Sexy, the preconceived idealization and a moment that required this epiphany
Sexy was not a word that I could not be
My mind a labyrinth of programmed media philosophy
Sexy was more than a body.
Sexy has become the new ideology
Sexy, the mind as it weaves and turns words into poetry
Sexy the sweet sensation of the fight to collapse the patriarchy
The way in which your body carries the soul of thee
Sexy, the encompassing idea of living authentically
Sexy, the intricate sensation of intellectual reciprocity
Sexy, the courage to reclaim it as part of my divine identity, not to define my femininity

Afrah Collier

Tokophobia

you should know that my body is not made for you - i am not right for miracles like you. it's not your fault or even mine; it's just that i keep thinking about how i have to pop myself like a balloon if you started to be real. i have to ice the swelling, double knot my laces so i don't fall into you. i can watch the strollers downtown and happy wives with glazed-over eyes as my friends coo about what it would be like to hold you. i fear i would drop you. i can't hold onto something that withers and shakes more than i do. i should crave you — it's biologically predetermined that i do but something got twisted in my DNA, and now the thought of you makes me weep. if you loved me - my heartbeat would rattle you to sleep. i want you to know that i could love if i tried. i just don't think my voice is made for singing innocence to sleep.

Sabryn Jones

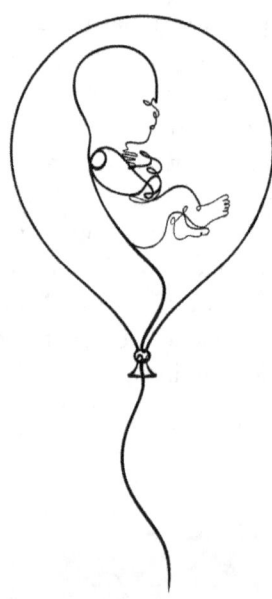

I surrender

I surrender myself to the passage of time,
As my skin weathers and wrinkles like bark,
Observing the gentle growth of fine, soft hair,
Glistening in the sunlight, winding toward the forest floor
May my breasts fill and nourish, then gracefully descend,
Towards the Earth, their nurturing source,
The fat on my body shall ripple, flow, and shift,
Embracing the years with the force of gravity,
Guiding my weakening flesh towards the ground,
To blend with the moss, mushrooms, and all life.
Drawing my being closer to its origin and final rest,
While my soul and life force ascend, reaching higher,
Towards the divine, the heavens, and the universe.
Stars and the moon draw near with every passing day,
I stretch, expanding from space to the Earth's core,
Transcending through all that exists and will ever be,
In this moment and for eternity.

Afton Doe

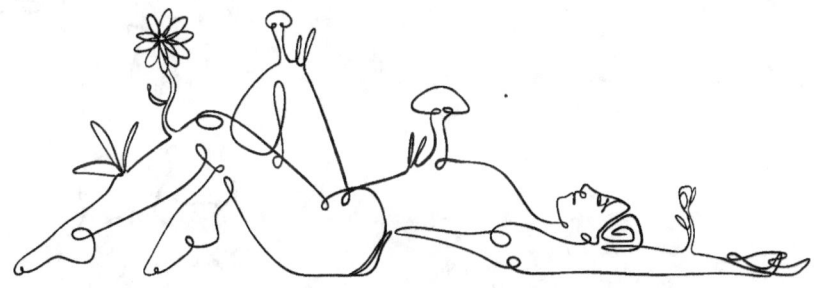

A Mother's Protection Spell

This year,
I chose perennial truths.
Like who gets to receive
This beauty my family blooms.
The efforts of sewing seeds
Of fruit and wisdom that tends wombs
Need not recognition akin to gold and jewels.
It's in the earth, in the soil,
In our breath, it is us.
From generation to generation
Degenerative disassociation
Is to be returned for earth's reclamation.
And only time will tell,
If the glass of wine spills
With eyes sinking deep into skulls
Or beam at the sparrows song to feel full.
Family is my greatest blessing.
And I speak these words
As if they were
A salt ring of protection.

Kelsey Klip

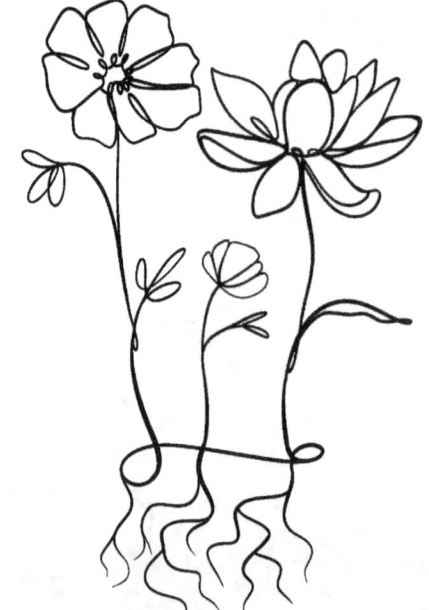

Opportunity

pawing at the door of opportunity
scratching, dry heaving
i will reach for you until the graceful tension in my fingers falls limp
and my outstretched arms succumb to gravity

would you love me just like this?
a puddle of a woman at your feet
my fragile body trained to dance for you
but she's not dancing right now
she's not writing either
i have too much to say to begin to write
i have too much memory stored in these hips to dance

how do i speak in prose when the words are not really words but
rather tide pools of emotion drowning me all at once
my lungs are too full of water to speak

tell me you love me baby
tell me the stage is my home
it leaves me broken every night, skin coloured blue from
proving my art to myself
everyone else already knows
i'm just waiting for her to see
i love you so much but you destroy me
and yet you are my greatest healing
like therapy every time i step into the light
every time i throw that guitar strap over my shoulder

Brooklyn Trapp

Laundry Sheets

Have you ever smelled the sweet allure of a memory?
A moment caught
wrapped in the subtly of fragrance, twisted and woven through time instantly?
A Sunday morning, sweet crisp breeze carries the traces of the lilac trees
The light catches crisply across our bodies wrapped and entangled in your bed sheets
Fingertips tracing the outline of your lips as your body stirs pleasurably
Hair dances across your face with the traces of last night's intensity.
Sweet, sticky, deep breaths as the waves crashed over me.
Laundry sheets
Your bed smelled of fresh laundry
Your eyes shone like amber honey and suddenly the encompassing feeling of clarity
It slid down my legs like nectar from a fruit tree
Laundry Sheets
The memory seeded in my mind so deeply. Sweet breaths of utter ecstasy, wrapped up in the moment leading to disparity.
Laundry Sheets
Letting go of you mentally
Moments of heartbreak given no clarity
The sound of your heart beat still pulsing in my memory
Laundry Sheets
Do you ever smell the glimpse of a memory?

Afrah Collier

Reset

If distance makes the heart grow fonder-
How can time heal all wounds?
Two weeks to flatten the curve
Three years of wars and headlines bombing the collective mind
Chosen family blown apart by
The News
False Dichotomy
Everyone knows DNA mutation occurs in the zygote cell, you
flat-earth mother-fucker
I swear we didn't always speak At each other in this way
I pinky-swear we used to speak To each other.

Grace Fay

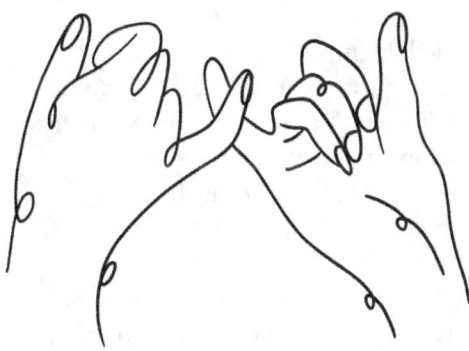

Unveiled Anthems:

Waterhorse

I carry my mother's breasts in my arms
The idea of her milk sang to me
Each dripping from the sagging breast of eternity

I carried my mothers rage into the tall grass of my rage
Cutting through lifetimes of surrounding forest
I poured her blood over filled sod prairie sage

I carried my mother's lungs in each of my hands
Until I could no longer hold their mass
Magnetic fields of dense grief crumbled into my surrender
Long child pressed blanket crying away the wind

I carried the weight of my mother's physical flesh
Its innocence wipers constantly
Excess skin and shame enveloping her waistline
The ghosts of vanity possessing the wellspring of her brilliance

I carried my mother's clit
In my favourite coat pocket - as a power stone of Gaia
Fidgeting with the smooth surface to release the origins of desire
A perplexed pleasure pulse
It surrounded me in a centrifugal force
Of pussy loving patterning

I wore my grandmother's emotional chaos around my neck
Her repressed tears wrapped in copper wire
Threaded with arbutus berries
Galactic clusters of blue combustion and choked back sound
Generational silence of the feminine animal rampage

I carry my mother's ancestors in the cornea of my eyes
As a beacon of her grandmother's sight and mine
A watchtower to witness the brave new world
of the women who won't shut up

The volcanic shorelines that she and I contain can only be accessed
by waterhorse
That I swear one day will be discovered

I carry my mother's breasts in the warmth of arms
Each containing the scriptures of duality
Quietude and death tingling on the tip of my tongue
Where nothing but the ancestors speak inside
My mind is the offspring
The byproduct of what they confide

Stevie Mud

whole again

infinite conversation and ideas
why is it that the flow never ceases
in stillness and laughter and
everything in between..
the sense that these are finally
all the missing pieces

L. Vallada

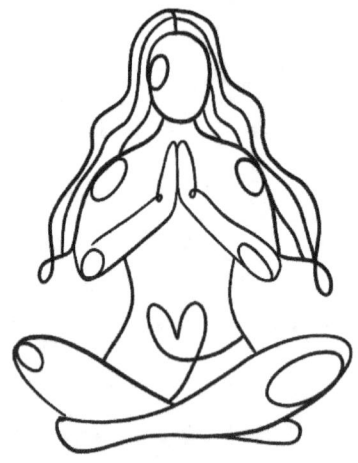

The Wilderness of my Truth

Maybe I'm not enough
Maybe I'm too much for you
Maybe my hands are too cold
And my heart too hot to hold

I thought you knew how to love a wilderness like me
Your long barren land longing for a seed

Yes, I'll flash my blood hungry eyes deep into your soul
And catch hold
Of the cracks that keep out the light
I won't be tamed when my presence sparks fire
Your self-doubt and insecurities may transpire
When my song shakes you to your knees
As I shatter the illusions
And make your wounds bleed
Unravelling the lies
The ties
To these illusions that don't serve my truth
To these illusions that don't serve you
I'm not limited to
Making myself small for you
Ill let my resounding howl wild and free
My sovereign soul
Roaming for all to see
No taming my wilderness
Though you'll still wonder in my tenderness
But it will not be me to persuade you of this undiscovered sanctuary

Monette Rockliff

Join our community!

Hey there! Womb bearer!
You too can experience connection,
And a brief sense of belonging,
Beyond the longing
The patriarchy provides,
For a low price of $99.99!
(That's my angel number FYI)
Oh wait, did you think
That cisterhood was free?
Well it's worth it, trust me.
Please pay your dues,
I paid mine too.
I know my worth.
And instead of branching out
To build a more sustainable option
For you and the hundreds of
  Women,
    Mothers,
      Sisters,
        Crones,
I will empty your pockets
To reveal the truth of all truths.
No snake oil I promise.
This is deep wisdom
From my ancestors bones.

I found the courage
To let down my walls
And repatriate another culture's knowledge.
And yes, I will be wearing only linen.
Beige linen, natural wools from my farm
On stolen land, never acknowledged.
I never surrendered my own freedom
Or these deep seeded beliefs
On these unceded territories.

The fields behind my land in winter
Is as white as the blank page,
White as the dark night that never came,
White as in "this is my ancestral right,
To pillage and regurgitate rituals that require
Rights of passage I have not walked but watched,
Package it up nicely and mail it over to you."

The consideration to diversify our space was considered
We just didn't have enough applicants.
And no, unfortunately there are no speakers
From where our retreat is held.
But we support them by giving them our business!
Because that's what we are,
We are a business.
Branded as wellness.
Branded as community.
Come now, be all you can be
For that sweet monthly fee.
Link in the bio

Kelsey Klip

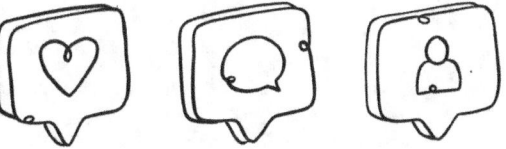

Power of the Tongue

I was taught to use my words but to use them only to please
To say only pleasant thoughts
And disregard my own needs
To craft beautiful words
To express very ugly feelings
As to not hurt anyone else
Just hurt myself
I'm dealing
With the repercussions of words never expressed
All the pain, anger and uncomfortable words left sitting on my chest
Never coming off never leaving
Scared to hurt the other person
Receiving
The hurt for myself the torment in fact
Now it's time to run all that shit back
Just practice saying it like it is
Not editing not overthinking not doing it for them
Baby this for you what you were always supposed to do
Take a hold of the power of the tongue that has been suppressed
Silence is too passive and gives the power to someone else

Jasmine Woodsen

Seasonal Contracts

Spare me the hope
I want your unsolicited honesty
Heavy though it may be
Bury me in the garden with it
Till the spring yawns
And my disappointment has turned over in the soil
Birthing a more resilient truth
Let me press up from the earth like a perennial:
Unapologetic
Here I am again, year after year
Blessing you with my seasonal bloom
Washed in dew
Awaiting your soft gaze
For you to bed down and hold me to your cheek
And breathe me in

And as we are all alive by the turning of this earth
Bound to our seasonal contracts
Something between us must necessarily die
As we bargain for our last moments of heat,
The sun charts its course across the sky
Pinching the horizon more with every turn

Will you mourn these dying days with me?
As the memories fade
Like the dusty ink of petals on a page
Captured and glued
Pressed between hard covers
But never the same spirit
As when our cells pumped with the beat of the earth

Will you sit with me and forgive what's left?

Jessamyn Stewart

Waves of Redemption: A Canadian Journey

Within me, anger and pain reside,
Urging me to unleash these stormy tides,
To engulf society, revealing truth untold,
Yet, hidden within, an illusion to behold.

These mighty waves, fearsome and wild,
But gentle souls shall be beguiled,
For beneath their daunting, destructive sight,
Lies serenity's embrace, washing darkness into light.

They approach these waves so grand,
To cleanse, to heal, across the land,
With truth, acceptance, and soothing balm,
Transforming hearts, bringing peace, and calm.

Together we shall ride these tidal swells,
As truth's power within us dwells,
The anger and pain, transformed to grace,
In these waves, a harmonious embrace.

Alexis Virus

Lunar Embrace

If I am being honest,
I yearn for nothing more than to feel the moon's soft glow,
tantalizingly slow across my bare bones.
My home tucked beneath the dark skies,
My spirit calls out to the night's endless sway,
seeking out one last dance in tonight's moonlit display.

I long to unravel my untamed desires,
To ignite a fire within, spreading desire,
With Luna's gentle guidance, I surrender to release,
Free to wander these streets where wildness finds peace.

Rebecca Ryan

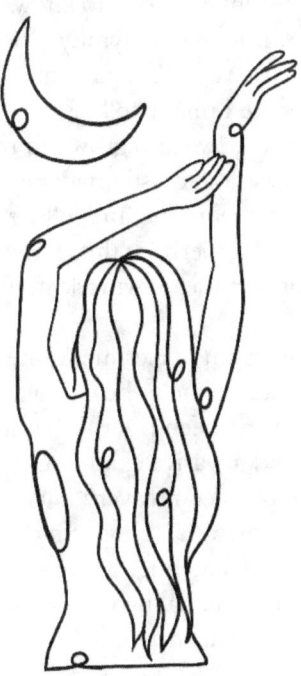

Somedays

Somedays, I feel like a wilted tulip:
Maintaining some semblance of strength and beauty while dying from the inside.
We wilted tulips have character and sprout hope, which is indispensable.

Somedays, I feel like a stranger in my own body
----- do you know what that is like? disjointed
   // bloody hell, mate

Somedays, I feel the need to put on a face while dissociating from the pain like a helium balloon escaping to the sky, just to participate in a society that doesn't have space for wilted tulips.

Somedays, I want everyone to know my pain and what I go through. Most days, I desire anonymity. I've only opened up about my health within the last year. Partially out of necessity for safety's sake to inform people I might collapse in a pain crisis unexpectedly while my vitals drop. I've also grown to realize the importance of spreading awareness and de-stigmatizing this complex disease. Since being diagnosed 10 years ago and telling a few close friends, they, too, have found that perhaps they have endo. No, it's not just a period, rather a brutal disease with deathly pain that isn't normal.

Somedays, my pain makes me want to die, yet it has also saved my life. It has taught me to be courageous and to trust my body. My pain has always been right. It has led to many ambulance trips, hospital stays, invasive exams, and, most recently, major surgery with a complicated recovery involving internal bleeding, clots, and a massive hematoma. Having a disease that mimics cancer, is invisible yet debilitating, grows anywhere in the body, yet is often treated as a hysterical byproduct of psychosomatic trauma, is a fucking patriarchal trip.

Somedays, I still question myself, as well as my pain, having been conditioned that pain experienced by anyone who is not cis and male is exaggerated and insignificant—even after ten years with a diagnosis and surgical proof. I have a higher pain tolerance than most, to the point of danger, and I don't notice when I get minor cuts or when my pain spikes— a bionic coping mechanism—the kind that wilting tulips grow to live with debilitating chronic pain.

Somedays, I feel like there's hope, like we are moving forward— which is precisely what we need most days.

Teresa Dorey

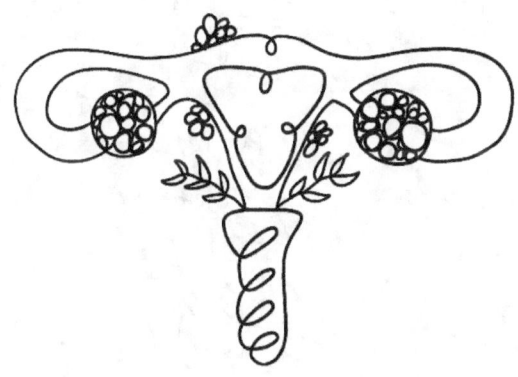

As With In

a man who has not yet
resolved his inner conflict
will destroy every woman
who tries to love him

Tanjeryne

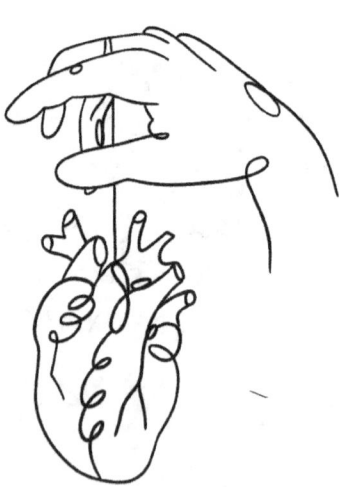

THE REVOLUTION

vibrating, myst-taking
these realms as finite,
in the ways we relate to our space.
atoms, bassed out, emanating
the souls access to divine light.
Don't close your mind in the face,
of the revolution.
in these hours, let your walls be the power
to point out exactly what your soul came here for.
why are you human?
what process does your desire bloom in?
get. un. lost. no matter the cost.
because all this, can't be for the money.
No, It can't be for the money.

CEDARS

SUPERWOMAN

They ask me what it's like to be a superwoman
To which I reply;
With a smile on my face,
Eyes radiating the warmest embrace
I say…
Do you know what it's like to die?

Do you know what it's like to be so sure of this life
Without never actually having an answer to the question why?

Where the place of uncertainty…
Is the only place you are certain of

Where the idea of eternity is the only concept…
More frightening than love.

You see my mama raised me to be strong
To think deep and stand tall
And when they slap you around,
You turn around and face another wall.

No matter the tears streaming down your face
Or paralyzing thoughts you can never erase…
Flashing memories of past mistakes,
With your body you learn to disconnect
Then reconnect
With just enough time for another step to take.

So you ask me…
From which fabric is a superwoman made?

You get to witness my beauty, my essence, my intelligence…

Lest we forget the complexity behind my tapestry
To which my magic has oh so much relevance.

What you see is the living document of the greatest story I will ever create

You see the human me…
The part you still believe
Had to die
In order for this Queen to be made.

Charlene Smith (a.k.a. Charlee Queen XO)

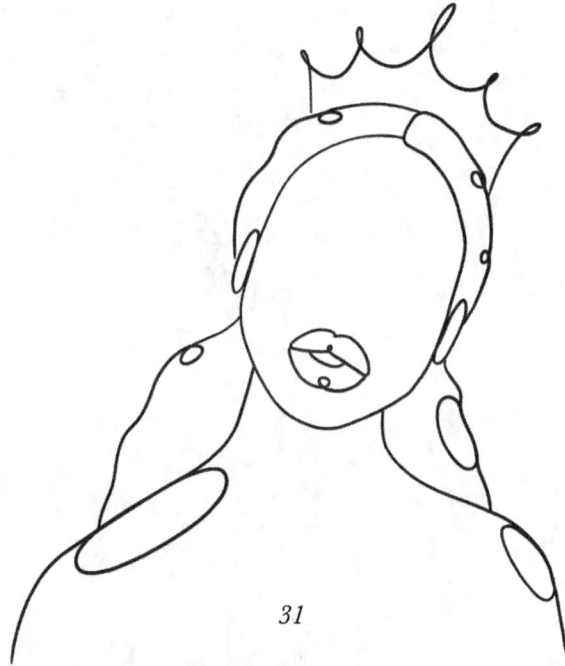

Intrusive Thoughts

I am going to gouge my eye out with a spoon. Not one of those plastic ones either, something nice and sturdy that can handle the weight of pressing on my optic nerve until it all goes dark. Or maybe it doesn't go dark. I don't know what happens when someone goes blind - I just know I am going to press until it ends. I imagine a bright gold spoon, only the best for the last thing I see. Maybe I'll do it on a sunny day in April, a day when the birds are so blue it hurts my eyes, and the
shadows are always late. I can't imagine it would cause much pain to have my capillaries burst open. Cold metal, the pop of the top of a dandelion. But then my phone alarm goes off, blaring Radar from the tiny speaker. The spoon drops from my hand and clashes into the bowl, spilling Cheerios all over the hardwood floor. Tiny perfect spheres.

Sabryn Jones

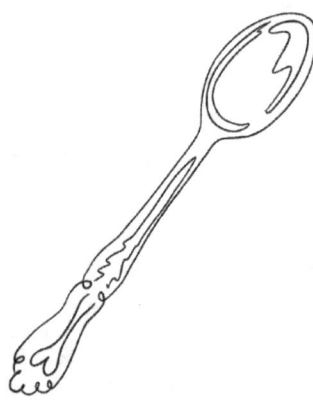

Untitled

I don't want to fall in love
I want love to greet me, smiling,
as I stand tall in my worth.
I want a love whose heat comes on slowly,
allowing me to surrender to the comfort of its warmth
I want love to hold a mirror up to me
Allowing me to gaze upon myself
with total acceptance

I am tired of fireworks, false promises and infatuation
I've learned that these whirlwinds often depart
as quickly as they've come
Leaving me to pick up the wreckage.
I recognize that in saying no
I am actually saying yes
to putting my needs first

I am not a lavish resort
ready to cater to the desires of those who drop in
Seeking escape from the monotony
of their day to day lives.
I am wild and all encompassing.
I feel in colour
I move with shape
and I think in abstraction.
I will not contort myself
morals fluid
to fill the cracks of another
An unworthy lover.

Gillian Peacock

Inner child love

I am in love
The reality is a stark contrast between fear and jubilation
Absolute Euphoria found in your eyes
Feelings of glee wrapped in your laughter
The overwhelming fear of losing all of this, tied to circumstance
Our story is anything but simple
Two broken children who found one another in the sandbox made from our pasts
Sliver-like grains of broken glass
Like pin pricks covering our childhood memories
enough to not look back
You are a jigsaw of everything I didn't know I needed
You seem to fit seamlessly into my heart and beautifully into my hands and I am here
Enraptured by you.

Afrah Collier

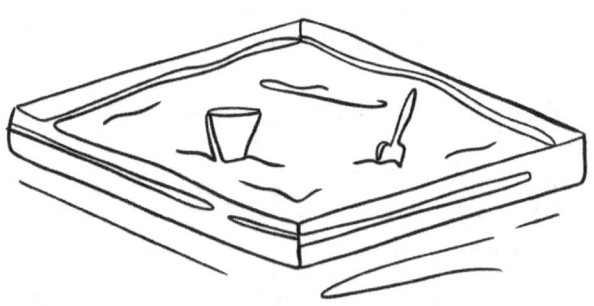

An unwelcome friend

Sometimes it seems as though only the darkness gets me
Unlike the world around me

What a lonely place to be
Friends with the dark
Suffocating my only tiny spark

Oh the ways she knows me,
Holds me,
And keeps me "safe"

Fearing the light will swallow me up
These Creature comforts
Won't let me get up

Sometimes I wonder how it must feel
To see with eyes that are real
And to escape her bitter touch

You ask me how I am
But she always knows
And I don't really want to expose
The truth to you

She's here sitting with me
Day after day
I'm still waiting for things to change,
And to find a new best friend.

Monette Rockliff

Becoming

I arrived at the altar of my own becoming
Tearful & enraged
Shedding stories from past lives
The ones my mother gave me
She would say:
We are a strong breed, this long line of women
Yet I found myself at the end of the family line
Soft & permeable
Always blowing in the wind
I learned to be strong
The way a calf learns to walk on new legs
But still, I grew up wild
Climbing trees to touch the clouds
Speaking in tongues
And rummaging for gold under canopies of lilac and pine

I grew up hungry for a kind of love I never had
Kissing boys at recess turned into years of heartbreak and longing for the unattainable:
Someone to hold all the pieces of me
Someone to show up unquestionably

Sometimes healing feels like re-injury
It feels like
Breaking bones to put them back into place
A place they've never been before
Muscles reforming to fit
To strengthen around my frame in new ways

These days
The spaces between what I say and what I mean have grown smaller
And the inner world within which I reside has grown richer and taller

As I deepen and grow
I surrender to the flow of where life wants to take me
Let my bones break
Shift & make me

And as the storms come
I hear the ancestors hum
Calling me back home

Like some unattainable wealth
I belong
To myself

Jessamyn Stewart

Medicine Chants

Linger in the liminal space
Where breath and consciousness mingle
Untamed intuitive knowing
Many sparks
Become one fire
Undulating tones and voices
Harmonize into soothing
Soundscapes
We sisters of song
Allow rhythmic sounds to heal
Digging deep into our spirits
Awakening the primal
We call to the pieces of our beings
The radiant soulful bits
Still ripe with creativity
Vibrant sparks of light and stardust
Coalescing into our highest selves

Carla Rae Taylor

My Politicized Body

nothing threatens
the structures of society
quite like
an embodied
woman

Tanjeryne

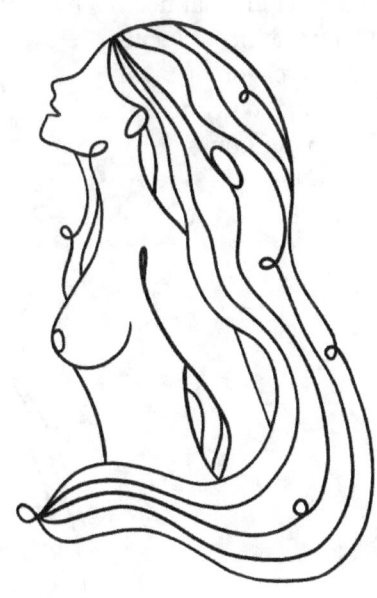

Scriptures on her bones

Never forget "what" you are
Nature's Law
Female
Supple milk tits
Possess the fertile glow
Swollen vulva don't you know
Gush with floods of blood
House the generations of stewards
I create to participate
I detest your rape
Don't rip my dress
And swipe the tampon to get my best
Your fear of me will not dominate me
I am not a machine that needs a battery
I am a being that needs security
I am the last creation of divinity
I am awakening to my deity
Scriptures on her bones

Lena Parnell

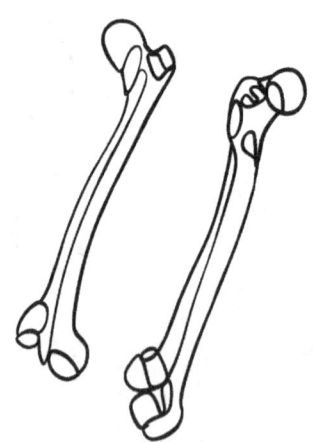

Pain Wars

Why, when I'm at my lowest
do you pounce on me
digging into me like a fierce lion
primal with anger
and not an ounce of love?

Are my feelings and truths
that triggering to you
that you must press
your anger and fear
right on my shattered heart?

The pain it activates in me
then I activate you
and it's a power play
of whose pain is greater

When I'm struggling on the inside
Why must I also fight you?
I'm already at war with myself
and then you bring on another attack
and it just makes me feel smaller
and smaller
until I feel I might just dissolve away into nothing

Aren't you supposed to be my safe place?
My refuge from the storm?
A lighthouse back to myself?

I just want this war to end.

Monette Rockliff

Wild Womxn/Reclaim HER

I used to be a mess. I used to deny myself liberation and entangle myself in the shadows of wounds, fear, and suppression. I used to oppress myself, as I was told that the very essence I carried within me, was full of shame. I used to hide and with this hiding bred inside a hungry animal. Starving for her own soul. Hungry for truth, hungry for expression, hungry for the raw, juicy pieces of herself that I kept shoving into a box, behind the big red curtain of conditioning and guilt for being HER.

I starved her of her gifts, her talents, her voice. I listened to her screams become whimpers lost to the layers of conditioning and lies that I built on her cage in the pushes to be "acceptable". I witnessed the way I needed to snatch the things I thought might feed my soul from desperation, only to find them out of alignment or integrity. Never satisfying for more than a moment. A slave to the impulsive rampaging. I watched this space breed from a place of constant self abandon and self betrayal. Never honouring my authentic yes or no. Too scared to speak my truth. Too scared to create boundaries. My childhood did not afford me the luxury of understanding any of these things, let alone empowered balance and alignment.

My mind was always estranged from the heart's intuition and truth. Like a patient with amnesia, completely unaware of her diagnosis. Only aware that she is not home and something seems to be amiss. A remembering of my original expression at the tip of the tongue, but always just slightly… out… of reach. What is it? Where did it go? Why did it go?

Always wondering where the hunger started and how on Earth I could ever find a way to satisfy it while walking in a haze. I used to feel condemned, wandering lost in my forgetting of being home inside myself or what home even was. I had no idea how to create safety or that it was possible. I had no conception of anything outside self doubt.

It was a lifelong brigade of trauma that led me down my path of remembering. As I began to heal through a series of deaths & rebirths, I began to see. As I deconstructed myself into chrysalis goo and re-emerged a butterfly over and over, I began to see more and more. Remember more and more. I remember every trap door. Every deception. Every purposeful misleading. I remember the moment the blindfold was given to me in my innocence and how I compliantly put it on, unbeknown the ones leading me weren't to be trusted as they downloaded a disempowered programming into me that as I grew, I learned to continue a way of being that led me further and further away from my own nature and grace. Away from my own alignment, away from my own wild womxn.

How much was taken from me. Through molestation. Through rape. Through abandonment. Through poor mental health structures and uneducated support systems. Through bullying, domestic violence, manipulation. Through the lies and secrets I was always told to keep. Through the way I was stigmatised to believe I was the one to carry the blame, shame and ick of trespasses. How I went on to trespass against myself in these beliefs. How I gave myself and my fire away over and over again to wet, cold hands without a second thought. Always beginning in unbridled hope and ending in the exploitation of my own beliefs of lacking worth.

What I have learned though, is insurmountable. What I have gained is incomprehensible. What I have pushed passed and emerged as is beyond anything I ever imagined. As I look back, I do find purpose in it all, regardless of whether or not it was "meant to be". It was. And I find so much value in all the experiences, I continue to find value in those experiences. I see how much wisdom and life it has afforded me to share with those who are seeking, healing and looking to validate hope within themselves. I see how much wisdom and LOVE it has afforded me to give to myself and this world. The depths of grief have bred depths of love through every ache, pain and gain of expansive being.

I feel blessed to understand the depth of my own sacredness and the sacredness of all life. I feel blessed for the second chances and gifts each day holds. I feel incredibly blessed to be alive and to FEEL. Everything I am experiencing and have witnessed is teaching me how deeply I FEEL and how much I really LOVE. I am in awe of the fire and magic I behold and the fire & magic I continue to see in everything around me. Even in those who have forgotten their own. I see it. I love that I see it.

So as I dance with scarred feet bare in the mud, with an infinite heart and open mind, I love all of HER. I remember. I reclaim myself. I see. Fuck, does it feels good.

Jaide Chyzyk

UNITE

All parts of me come into one.
Embracing the dark side of me that no one can see;
Duality is my nature,
I love both sides of me.
Once I accepted all of me, I became Free.

Nadine EL-Hajj

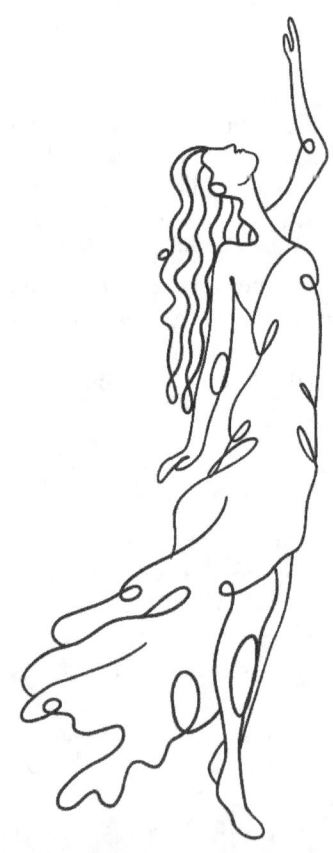

Beast

Here, I stand on the edge of your moon, screaming your name.
Amidst the transitional April Sun
I want to undress for you and watch this curiosity trickle down my breasts
As I cry to the beast in you

Your bite has infected my heart
What do you cry to in pure darkness, when you beg for eternity?
Which man has brought you to such reason, that you weep in his memory each rising?
Who has reached inside your chest, with their bare hands, and stopped your heart?
And which voice, which body was able to bring you back to life?

Do we beg for the same creator? Or are they siblings, recreating themselves as separate illusions so that you and I can come together?
I found this longing in the dirt of your essence. You've planted seeds and cliches I want to devour.
This pecking bird, that I am.
This lavish indulgence in seeking a cure for mortality.

There is a detriment within the animal I incarnate,
The strident dialogue that has burdened me.
You've come here.
Traveling miles from down the street.
Loving dedicating to the many fatigued women floating behind my eyes.

I am a house head – where the entrance is ajar.
A constellation mind – my craters a stoic acid wash.
I am a silk moon – descending from a lineage of women's heaping spoons of regret.

I'll pry inside of your weary bones, and make an elegant nest of my hair.
I'll make love to you so tragically, your flesh will transform into hide.

Stevie Mud

Embers of the Untamed

a hard bird to cage
a tough fire to put out
the dove dances
through flames
we find beauty
in raw places

Tanjeryne

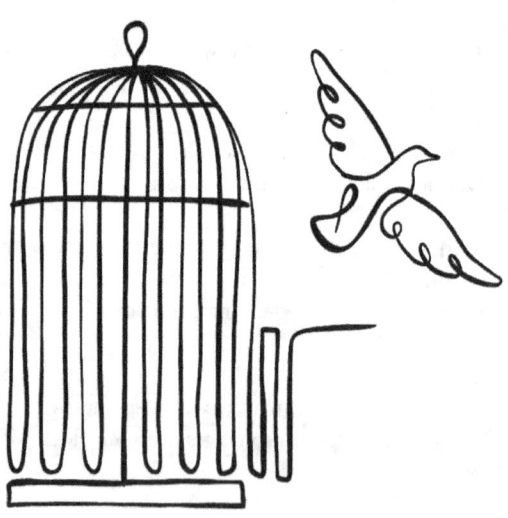

Authenticity

Authenticity.
Like liquidity, the sweet heat of whiskey
as it unfurls itself within me.
I love authenticity.
Stimulate me cerebrally.
Tingle me till knees buckle
from the warmth of your ability to be present.
Let naked words drip from your tongue down my spine, sending
shivers to my fingertips.
Let the heat of your breath raise the hairs
on my neck as you look into me.
Authenticity.
How you have me wrapped around your finger,
moving me in a pleasurably slow linger,
back and forth in rhythmic surrender -
Oh authenticity.
Please me with your words revealing layers of your intricacy,
your complexity.
Allow me to dive deep into the ocean of your experience.
When you look at me with eyes unclouded by layers
of who you think you should be...
I melt.....
Sweet sticky me running down my leg -
Oh authenticity.

Isabelle Desrochers-Stein

ImagINatiONs

Playing with
The spectrum ends
Pendulum
Seeking balance mends

In on
Up around sideways
In between
Underneath
Everywhere
All the ways

Light… Dark
Colour… Shades
Bright… to Dim
Appear… then Fade

Dom
Sub
Hate
Love
Dull
Sharp
Below
Above

Opposites.
Duality.
Living & Fatality

Mass Confusion
Inner Calm
Age of Aquarius
Or world war Bomb

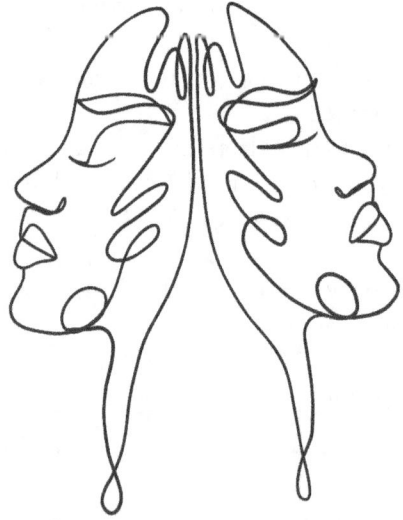

A Symphony of Women's Voices

Directions though
Become less on the ends
More of a circle if the
Line instead bends

If I start in the east
And walk to the west
I'd come back to the same
In the positioning quest

So then round I go
To define where's the middle
How many Circulations
One ponders the riddle

Walk the circle, Walk the line
It is balance I'm seeking
Takes a bit of nudging,
Reflection and tweaking

And in middle
Which is always in motion
I find the true path
Of my inner devotion

But it only exists
Because contrast
Paradox
Time like a clock
It only unlocks

That neither becomes
Without the other
Timelessness
In this prayer for our mother

Zoii Topia

A Mother's Reprise

Your eyes,
the way they pierce and dance,
so deep, so bold.
Stolen moments as they curiously yearn for all there is to know.

Your tiny fingers,
delicate, like a mallet slowly gliding 'round a singing bowl.
Nothing compares to the feeling inside as they wrap around my own.

Your beaming smiles tug on my heartstrings,
they've filled every void,
my heart is whole.
Each one bestowed upon me is a vision to behold.

Your warmth,
envelops me in hope when life feels beyond my control.

While your laugh,
a melody of pure joy,
is the only song to soothe my soul.

For my darling, Sonise.

Kayla Hastings

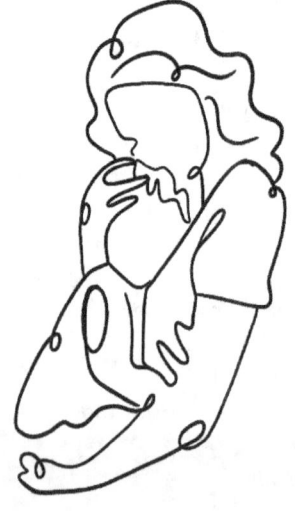

My Eyes Are Closed

My eyes are closed
To all the light
My ears can't hear
What's true or right.

I'm blocked with pain
From past mistakes
My heart is cold
My body aches.

And so I must
Delve into fears
Face emotions
From early years.

The work is hard
Sometimes in vain
To dig down deep
Exposes pain.

And yet there comes
When wounds stripped bare
The chance to heal
To breathe new air.

J.Hildebrandt

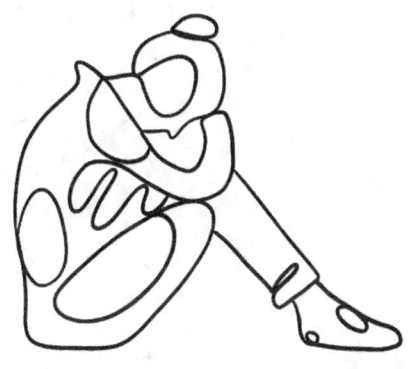

Projection

I feel her judgment
With blood hungry eyes
I realize
Its not me
Its her
That I stir
The wild within her
She hidden

Monette Rockliff

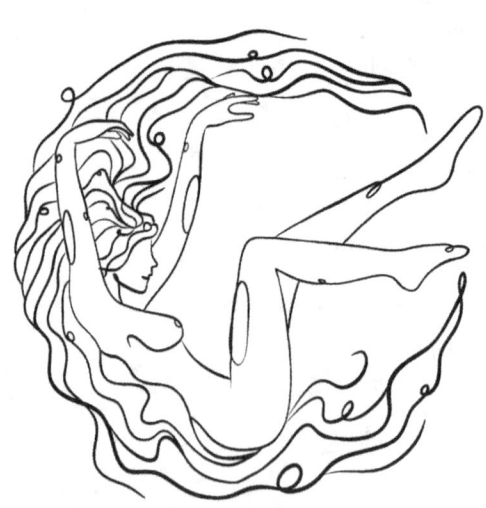

Dark Goddess

Fill me with your fingers, dark goddess
Below the bottom chamber
Where the maidens hold each other in secret
Open them full inside and spit them circling into blossom
Every piece of knuckle and nail shoved deep
Until I'm split open
Each hunk of flesh, spiraling me wet and bloody
Back into pieces of formation blocks
Where each flap of flesh
An erotic mess of shrieking woman birthed from their
torn apart grief
Pussy ravaged with every sister's dark fierce madness
Her fingers of lace ribbons,
Binding me to my deepest fears
Claws like sand dollar stories
The entire seabed crumbling in the painful death-rebirth
of aloneness
Shredding every piece of sanity
Leaving me humiliated to negotiate with her shadows that
won't go so easy
Shall I live and serve?
I beg for her to spin my life into lotus blossom
She drops moon secrets the louder I scream

Stevie Mud

mother

they're trying to erase the feminine
we've seen this all before
from the witch hunt to the word cunt
the attempt at stealing our power
the erasure of my nature
the eradication of my sisters
it's something they can never do, actually
to be woman, is the closest you can be to god
i am not a birthing person i am your goddamn mother
sit when i ask you to
listen when i speak
put some respect on my name
on her name
a mother doesn't need you but goddamn you needed a mother
she is creator not creature
my pussy is your maker
my cum is the OG psychedelic
my placenta your home
keep your hands to yourself
keep your laws out of my body
don't bite the breast that fed you.
i fucking created you
and in the same breath i will fucking destroy you

Brooklyn Trapp

Dancer Unveiled

Sensual soulful beats
Unfurl at my feet
Falling as rose petals
Harmonies persuade

Surrendering to the music
I become the dance
I never knew I could be
Edgy, sacred, beautiful
Entirely me

I toss the lance
My hero's ego crumbling
Brought to my knees
Unwavering
Never stumbling

Open heart
This truth becomes me
The bodice of fear, shame, guilt
Now shed
Raw in my power
I dance
I glow

Carla Rae Taylor

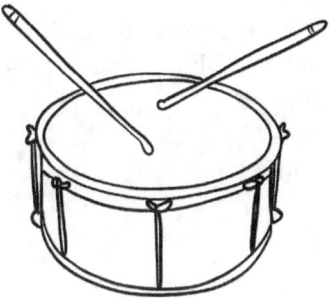

Forgiveness

To forgive is to realign with the divine plan God has in mind
To rise above all earthly laws
No space
No time
And experience the bliss
That is a gift of presence inside

I forgive you
I forgive me

For every word misspoken in reflection of our crazy

To be the alchemist of the sky,
Of the land,
Of the sea
And realize that like the trees,
We transmute the energy into synchronicity.

Please
Believe

No, not hope.
But create your faith in the unseen.

For hope is simply despair doubtful of the dream
Laced with the false inclination that the creation is someone else's responsibility?

But it's you
It's me
It's us, it's we

To walk forth into the promised land that the king had once dreamed.
And me?

Well, I'm a Queen.

Adorned by my ancestors,
Still feeling the pain that we bleed.

To look in the eyes of our oppressor
And smile knowing that we're free?

Man this forgiveness shit ain't easy...

My body still scarred and face still marred
From the lashes of your words and chains on my heart

But again... My heart still beats and my mind still mends.

My Forgiveness.

As I put aside all the hate knowing that you are just a reflection.

No need for remembrance.

For they say hell hath no fury like a woman scorned
Well I say
That in hell I'll play
So with the rise of my kin
A new heaven is born.

Charlene Smith (a.k.a. Charlee Queen XO)

Short Talk on Loneliness

Did you hear that loneliness is hereditary? My parents were lonely even when they were married. I felt the loneliness creep into the holes of my bones until it became all I ever was. I was never alone but I was always lonely. I found loneliness in my kindergarten classroom corner. Gripping construction paper until my knuckles paled. I was the runt of the litter, and someone always has to be left to die. Loneliness takes shelter in the apartment building that caught fire years ago and the city hasn't done anything to remove – it stays half burnt and half alive. The graveyard on the side of the road that nobody drives into anymore but the kids swear it's haunted. You are alone. You always will be. Loneliness looks like the abandoned shoe on the highway, lying on the side of the street like roadkill. You don't know if you want to be the shoe or the dead thing. Both belonged to something bigger once – both had more than you did. When loneliness becomes your only friend, you begin to search for it at parties. In the bottom of red solo cups, sticky floorboards, you go to bed with it in cold, itchy sheets and wake up alone. I've learned to love the loneliness – to see some mangled beauty in the twisted remains left behind. I sit with loneliness at my dining room table by the window. We feel the sun on our skin as it seeps in with warmth. Loneliness reaches across the wooden slab and takes my hand in theirs. I grip so tightly onto their hand, unwilling to let go.

Sabryn Jones

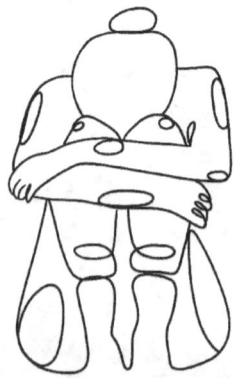

Once my Gala

My encouragement brings,
An upheaval of warmth from her chest.
You can see a doorway, a portal between her breasts.
And only I can feel the frequency when the excited particles
give way.

Now, I can't believe the divide, the separation between our eyes.

Once constructing a constant stare - a fused gaze into eternity.
It has become a crumbling structure beyond god's measures.
It was made of all the parts of her hands.

Stevie Mud

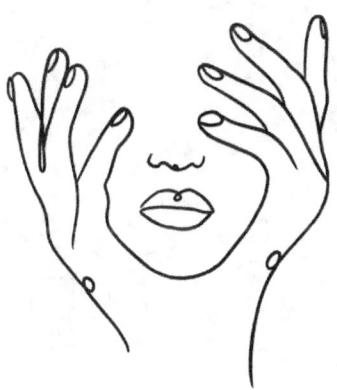

Unveiled Anthems:

Nature VS TRANSHUMANISM

Lack of Mortality * Drag Show Story hour
Lack of Ethical Leadership * Dominance Culture Censorship
Lack of Principles * Human Rights VS Nature Law
Lack of Evolution * Beliefs VS Immutable Truth
Lack of Vision * Propaganda Screen Time
Lack of Prosperity * Monetary System
Lack of Purpose * No Meaning
Lack of Fathers * Logical Structure
Lack of Mother * Kin Unity
Lack of Village * Knowing The Way
Lack of Love * All the above

Lena Parnell

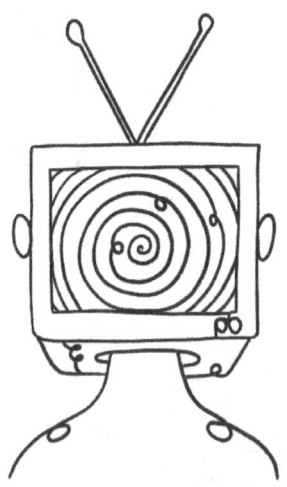

I can hear my shadow

I breathe in
Breathe out
Shake away the pain
Settle my self doubt
I know I'm better than this
I can hear my shadow
Calling me down
It thinks I'm safer where I no longer wanna hang around
Oh I know this as my comfort zone
It's true I've only ever known
The places I have been that I've now outgrown
And I'm ready, ready to call myself back home
To the place that lives inside
I reside
As unfold every little crease
Every bit of crunch, the ick, the stick,
The gunk
I lean in cause I know it's where I begin
To find the gifts
The gifts I've been hiding away
Under all the ways I didn't know any better
I fall back in love with myself
With a clearer vision
And a mission for health
Like I've never known it before

Jaide Chyzyk

THE TENSION

When we blink, Shift in the slate
Of my gaze, For the release
Move this let it dissipate
The holding in the wait
For an idea as foreign to our realities
Innate to the technicalities
Of the chase in the wake of being
I did not come here to manipulate
Any resistance in your existence
Within mine
No boy, I thought you were of my kind
Willing and reading, present and seeing
Craving to participate in something bigger
Then the crash lines, energetic finite
The flow in and out of my mind
Curious and child like exposed to the cosmic minds eye but reality sits
And the truth of this matter is
You don't ask me questions anymore
You haven't engaged in my mind in weeks
Cruel in your no speak
Letting me run circles in your supposed
expressed reality
Nah bro, this type of shit is too far from me.
I gave you every opening
The house of my heart a patio for being
Full of air, intention of a freely navigating
Scenario for you
Following the tip of this thread
Clarity seeps in.
Like a tea stain on my favourite dress
If you can't talk to me about your process, about your being. About your needs and your boundaries
Then in this with you, I can not be.
I can't meet you anywhere,
Without relating, giving me the courtesy
navigating what is showing up to you in respect.
I'm not a child. I'm not interested in games.

Guessing and messing with values, the testing
No boy, that shit is not for me.
Be clear, don't speak backwards.
You know that you're doing it.
If all eyes are watching, yours are the ones that really see.
Exactly what is your heart's priority
Hold me at a high enough regard
To release me, the vibrations I feed you
Don't conceive me into believing
Your words hold their integrity
If they don't.
Not a placeholder. Not a nice idea.
I am infinity in love in my offering to the being
Of whose I fill their cup
My water is the ocean deep and mystic
Life giving supporting the harmony yet realistic
To who can swim and who will drown.
The land walkers have their reasons.
I can settle with this. But under my skin is this idea
You would let it sit speechless
Salted sea in your mouth
Floating beside you, I tried to.
Give you all the space to let me know
Exactly what it is that you needed
The void in this only you created
I'm not looking for love
That feels like I'm so far away from that being.
I feel far away from mostly everything in my waking experience
In this moment, I feel really far away from you.
For the first time, And I don't know what to do.
I'm not looking to feel out of place
I'm of interest in a safe space
For my moon.
Right now, your arms, no. It's not with you.

CEDARS

The Sorceress

She
The Sorceress
Lyrical mistress to the underground flow
Imploding with love as she draws back her bow
Three silver arrows she'll aim at your heart
As they pierce they'll heal anything broken apart
Flood you with warmth, illuminate with light
Bring dawn to the edge of your dark eternal night
A truth unfolds under wing of fire
Unearthing the wonders of the mother land's desire
Secrets told in whispered tones
Walking on layers and layers of bones
The voice of the forest speaks of her light
She gives power to dream in lucid flight
Taking steps upon the woodland path
The moon but a sliver
She comes upon a riddler and his poetic wrath
Never to reveal what's left in her quiver

Carla Rae Taylor

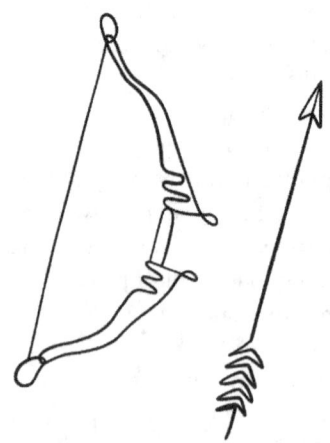

REBIRTH

What I see in front of me is what I am to be.
I AM free,
Not only can I see, but I can also feel.
Like a symphony, all my senses speak to me.
A beautiful harmony,
This beauty had always been right in front of me.
Not knowing that I convey the power to see, feel, or hear.
Not until a year ago, even more just a few days ago.
My lenses got cured and purified from all the debris.
The eye has always been watching me; only I had been made not to see.
If I knew then what I know now,
This time here, for me, would never be.
Thus, an unseen force led me onto the unknown path to return to where I originated.
Back home; A Home Return.
Returning to the presence of overwhelming peace and bliss,
I then understood the meaning of "Inner Happiness Is Bliss."
Through this experience, I realized the purpose & importance of such wise words
have always been, & are still missed.

Nadine EL-Hajj

Women's Day POEM

To be a woman is truly something special
Having birthed a nation
And given life to its people
yet still not its equal…

I could never quite understand.

Just how a woman could give him life
and yet still be second to a man?
No.

I don't understand.

How the very space of life's containment,
Can be taken
And misshapen,
Dismissed significance simply for your erotic entertainment.

We are your mothers
We are your sisters
We are your lovers
And we are your friends

And before all this,
We've been the Empresses and Queens dressed in the finest of silks and linens.

So I gotta ask this question.

Is the struggle real?

Or simply consciousness in expression?

Can we quantify what we feel or simply take it as a lesson…

A Symphony of Women's Voices

Ohhh
Such feminine presence

Swirls around me like a tide

And no matter the lightest of tone
Or the richest of melanin
It feels good to look around and see my reflection from the inside

Nowhere to hide.

So I stand tall
And I raise my hand
To pay homage to every woman upon whose shoulders on which I stand,
Yes,
Thank you ma'am

For all your strength and sacrifice you've made, it's true.

And I know that every time I speak and my voice is heard
the divine essence I feel in me,
Is you.

Charlene Smith (a.k.a. Charlee Queen XO)

I think about forever

In the depths of slumbers embrace
A melody resides
Filling sacred space
It tugs my heartstrings wide
Notes resound longingly inside
Something lost to time
Leaves me mystified

Within me it stirs
Echos in heart chambers
Songs whisper
Breathes life into a beat
Rattles bones
Something deep

Visions of ceremony come through
Weaving prayers for the youth
A tune so resolute
The wisdoms takes root

A song long trapped
Caught & caged
Made a home in my bones
Like a nesting sparrow
Nestled into the marr
Life cycles unfolds
Telling stories untold

Kavita Sundar

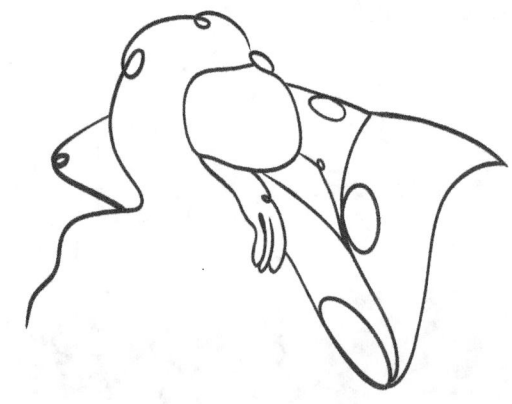

Generational Curses

I am not the first woman to break generational curses
But I have learnt that it is okay to walk away
From relationships that no longer feed my soul
I will not stay
Because my great grandmother, grandmother and my mother did
I have made a promise to myself that I will never
Be in a relationship or marriage
That dims my light
And if I am lucky enough to have a daughter
I will tell her that the most important love to give
Is the love that she gives to herself
That a man is no more than his actions
And that words are empty promises
That expectations lead to disappointment
Because when shit breaks the fan
She'll be the only one putting those broken pieces together herself.

Amani Assaf

Enthralled

The darkness inside me has a mind of its own,
And it took me a long time until I realised that her
Thoughts were never my own.

Oh she was convincing,
The darkness,
Never ending,
She sowed within me
Seeds of insanity,
Sprouting toxins,
Blooming malice.

Her endlessly persistent,
Persuasive ideas had slithered their way into the
recesses of my mind..

Her forked tongue,
Whispered perversions,
Gaslighting me into submission,
Kneeling before her falseness,
Revelling in the uncertainty,
The naivety,
The brutality of her love.

My sanctuary,
Lay sullied,
Made into her throne,

I,
made into a fool.

Rebecca Ryan

To be Woman

the cool thing about being a woman

is my strength presents itself as softness
you won't know you've been bitten by the serpent until she's
watching you writhe beneath her pretty feet
because the bite of your flesh tasted like the kiss of an angel
the venom unassuming
her calculated touch so soothing
she's well read
well fed
well learned
she doesn't care to be understood
in fact she doesn't care too much about anything
except for animals
and bugs
and the ocean
and poetry
and the general knowing that quantum entanglement exists and is
supporting her universal desires

okay so she actually cares about a lot
what a beautiful problem to have
to know so many things to care about
it's one thing to love
but it's another completely to be loved by her
the giving without taking
with every touch her heart aching
red lipsticks got your heart breaking
fuck
to be woman

Brooklyn Trapp

Metamorphosis

In the silence of this cocoon
We reflect infinite imagination
Creation dissolving
Into fluid formation
All that has been
Now redefined in the process
Rain drop into the ocean
Illuminated womb of devotion
Call forth fresh eyes
Clear mind
Let. Life. Rise.
From the ashes of hope
For love may always be
Resurrected
Rights of passage mark
The transformation of perspective
Connected
To a bigger picture
That offers a vision
To strive beyond fear
To make. It. Count.
Whole of soul
There is no doubt
Only curiosity
For this mystery
That keeps us in awe
When we witness the pause
Between. Each. Beat.
Let Earth kiss your feet
And bring you home
Where we belong
To this moment
As a heart that is free to love
And be the alchemy of
Our collective
Metamorphosis.

Sophia Ocean

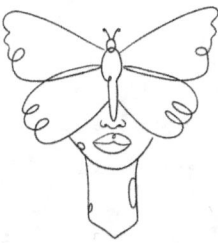

Thank you for taking the time to read our poems.

www.ingramcontent.com/pod-product-compliance
Lightning Source LLC
Chambersburg PA
CBHW071109240526
45469CB00006BD/2411